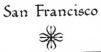

WHEN THE MANY BECOME ONE

Three Lectures

SWAMI ASHOKANANDA

Vedanta Society of Northern California

2/98

ISBN 0-9612388-1-X

This book, originally entitled My Philosophy and My Religion, *contains three lectures given by Swami Ashokananda at the Vedanta Society of Northern California in San Francisco. The first two, originally entitled "My Philosophy and My Religion — I" and "My Philosophy and My Religion - II," were delivered, respectively, at the Old Temple on April 22, 1956, and at the New Temple on December 10, 1961. The third lecture, "When the Many Become One," was delivered at the New Temple on December 3, 1967. The verbatim transcripts of all three lectures have undergone only such editing as is needed in transposing the spoken into the written word.*

A VIEW OF VEDANTA — I

I SHOULD TELL you at the outset that Vedanta is a vast system of thought and experience, so vast that I think rarely can anyone claim he has fully comprehended its depth and extent. In fact, I do not think it was meant that everyone should fully comprehend this philosophy or experience all its truths; rather it was expected that out of this vast system each would take what he thought best suited to himself. It was not produced by one person but by hundreds and thousands of people experimenting upon metaphysical truths, and it is the aggregate of all the findings of these people. It may even be said that the search for these truths has not yet ended. It is quite possible that other things will be added to Vedanta as time goes on, making it more and more perfect, more and more comprehensive.

Under these circumstances, I don't think you will wonder that a sincere seeker of truth should find in Vedanta his own individual ideal or that he should study it in his own individual way; he might be convinced of certain parts of its truth for instance, and find his own arguments and justifications for accepting them. I had some such thought in mind when I chose this subject, and I shall try this morning to tell you something of my particular understanding of Vedanta.

1

First I should tell you that of the general principles of the philosophy and religion of Vedanta it
is monistic Vedanta that appeals to me most.
But I do not on that account find myself antagonistic to the other interpretations, the theistic
interpretations of Vedanta; I like those also. I do
find, however, that I cannot remain fully satisfied with theism.

You understand what theism is. Theism holds
that God is separate, or at least distinct, from the
individual soul, and the general approach of a
theist is that of devotion to God and of service to
God; his ultimate ideal is a sort of union with
God in which the distinction between himself
and God is not obliterated. There have, of
course, been theists who in their own experience
have found this distinction being obliterated,
but their attitude to such obliteration is not the
same as that of the monist. They give little im-
portance to it; they regard it as simply an
intensification of their devotion and generally
speak of it as an intense love of God which
makes them forget themselves. After all, in an
ecstasy of joy you may lose consciousness of
yourself. Therefore they do not believe that one
would be justified in thinking that this obliteration constitutes a fundamental revelation of
truth, as do the monists. A monist thinks that

this obliteration is proof that the distinction between the self and God, even in its highest form,
is part of relative reality, part of the realm of
ignorance; that is, he maintains that the disap-
pearance of this distinction is proof that the
highest reality is an indefinable identity. This is
the basic difference between the monist and the
theist.

Of course, from this difference follow other
differences—differences in approach and in
practice. A theist never tries to think that every
person is God; he would say, "Yes, God dwells in
the heart of everyone," or "All are the children of
God," but he would not think that every person
is God Himself. That would appear to him some
sort of blasphemy. While no Hindu would hold
that souls were created by God, Hindu theists
believe that, though the souls exist eternally,
they are still distinct from God and that that
distinction will never be removed. The monists,
on the other hand, hold that the ultimate reality
is only one; if you see many realities—many
different souls and beings—that is due to your
ignorance.

Ignorance does all kinds of strange things. If
by some mischance it happened that man could
never turn his head upward so that he could
never see the sun, then I imagine he would think
there were many suns because he would find
them in many bodies of water. He would see

"suns" in the thousands and thousands of dew-
drops on the lawn, in pools, in the sea or in
rivers, wherever there is water or anything that
could reflect; and I imagine he would actually
believe that innumerable luminous objects exist
here, there, and everywhere. We don't make that
mistake because we can turn our heads upward;
we can look at the sun and so have no doubt that
all the many "suns" we see on earth are reflections of the one sun. The monists claim that the
same is true of the many fragments of consciousness we see here. It is true that in some—
in trees and plants and the lower orders of
animals—this consciousness seems almost
dormant: we find the working of life, but we
cannot say we find signs of consciousness.
Nonetheless, wherever there is consciousness,
or a suspicion of consciousness, the monist
claims it is, as it were, nothing but the reflected
sun—that is to say, there is really only one consciousness.

I must tell you, in order not to mislead you,
that even the monists have held two different
views on this point. While some have said there
is only one consciousness and all the other con-
sciousnesses that you see are just reflections of
this one infinite consciousness, or Brahman, or
Divinity, others have said that one and the same
consciousness has, as it were, become divided by
this infinite number of forms and appears as an

infinite number of fragments of consciousness. There has been a lot of philosophical disputation between these two schools, and those who want to think they are not party to the quarrel hold that the second view, the fragmentation-of-consciousness-by-the-forms view, is the lower explanation of individual souls, whereas the other, the reflection theory, is the higher explanation.

But whatever their differences, all monists are agreed that all these conscious beings, as well as this world, which is generally considered to be insensate, are one reality. If you think that God also exists, supervising these many souls and this universe, then the monists say all these three entities, which generally form the subject matter of philosophical systems, are really one. In fact, since you could not even speak of "one" unless there were distinct realities of some kind, and since in this ultimate there are no distinctions, they say that you cannot even speak of it as one. Nor can you speak of it as two or as not-one; so sometimes they say, "He is devoid of the sense of the one and the sense of the not-one." You really cannot speak of Him—Brahman—in any terms at all; that is what they mean. But for practical purposes we can say there is one reality. That is the basic proposition of monistic Vedanta.

Now, you may ask, "What about me? This

philosophy seems to do away with me. It explains everything away; I who am seeking the truth, even I am eliminated." It is as though you had gone to a great philosopher asking him many questions, and instead of answering all these questions he took a stick and tapped you on the head and put you out of the discussion. It almost seems like that kind of philosophy. But I should tell you that the monists also say that I who am questioning and seeking this truth, I am identical with this one Reality. If you say, "Then what about the outside world—the world that we see?" In the highest experience the outside world does not exist at all, so we do not have to think about it in relation to the ultimate. In that experience there is only one Self, one Reality; each feels identified with Brahman or Divinity. It is a strange kind of situation, which has very little to do with our present state of existence. Here our existence is spelled out in terms of distinctions—distinctions from one another and from the world of objects. We seem to think that we couldn't exist if we were not distinct from others, that we couldn't act unless we had insensate things as objects. The monists claim, however, that this situation—this present way of thinking and knowing—is itself a product of ignorance. A higher state of knowledge and a higher state of existence is identity, even though it seems to be almost antagonistic to our present state of knowledge and our present mode of knowing. But then, who does not know that knowledge is opposed to ignorance?

We find it difficult to persuade ourselves of this truth, but nevertheless it is the truth: ultimate Reality is of the nature of pure consciousness beyond all distinction, all division. Lest you begin to think that it sounds awfully dry and abstract, the monists remind us that this consciousness is not only infinite being, it is at the same time infinite joy. Joy you can define in various ways: joy is also love; joy is beauty and sweetness; joy is peace; so it is really all that you want. It might be said that this pure consciousness is the fulfillment of all our values, or *arthas*, as we say in Sanskrit. There we find fulfillment of everything we are seeking here. So pure consciousness is not abstract; it is a thoroughly substantial reality. Nothing is rejected, nothing is lost in the realization of the final identity; on the other hand, everything that is incomplete and imperfect here is realized in its utter completeness and perfection there. The obliteration of distinctions, of the individuality of things, is in reality an obliteration of imperfection. Separation is a sign of our imperfection, of our bondage. Just as if many friends had each been locked in a solitary cell and could not communicate with one another, so we as limited individual souls have been, as it were, put into cells and separated from one another. You must admit that that is not a desirable state of things. Freed from all these limiting forms and limiting thoughts, we realize ourselves as identical, and in that we find utter fulfillment of ourselves and utter fulfillment of everything that is in our universe. That is the ideal of monistic Vedanta.

But when you think of the limited individual as he is now—and in considering any philosophical system you should think of him—you will find that in monism he is regarded in this way: through mischance he has become identified with a fragment of mind which he calls *his* mind and a fragment of matter which he calls *his* body. This identification comes through ignorance of his own true nature, and it is maintained by that ignorance. In fact, this identification is both the cause and the effect: this ignorance is perpetuated, or made continuous, because of our identification with the body and the mind, and this identification occurs originally because we are ignorant. The problem can therefore be approached from two different points of view: From the religious aspect of Vedanta you could act in terms of the knowledge that you are not the body and not the mind (which is, of course, a classical practice); or from the philosophic aspect, you could hit at the root or cause by directly knowing yourself as what you truly are, pure consciousness, or Spirit, thereby getting rid of the effect, identification with mind and body. Either way, you realize yourself as the pure Spirit even while apparently living in the body.

Generally speaking, in Vedanta the tradition has been to go to a qualified spiritual teacher and to hear from his lips these grand truths. It was always considered that the words of such a person had a special power about them, the power of penetrating through all the barriers that seem to be in the minds of those who are ignorant and of awakening in them a sense of conviction about the truth. If you hear the truth from someone who has not realized it even partly, although he may adorn his theme with beautiful language, it will leave you cold; you will find that it has not had any effect at all so far as your own mind is concerned. But when you hear it from a qualified teacher, an illumined soul, something is awakened within you, and that something will go on waking you up—more and more—until you find that all your ignorance has vanished away.

There are, indeed, monists who say that all that is necessary is to hear this truth from the lips of a teacher: the rest will take care of itself. But others say that more is required; when you hear this truth you must then think about it, you must take hours and hours to think about it. There are also books written on these subjects, and on the basis of these holy texts you think about the truths you have heard from your teacher. Then, when you have doubts, you ask him about them; or you can find in the texts of Vedanta the answer to these doubts. But if you can ask your teacher, that is the better way; for he will remove your doubts. Finally, when your mind can no longer raise any doubts, it is forced to accept this truth. And such is the nature of truth that once you are convinced it *is* the truth, you cannot ignore it; it becomes part of your being. Even in ordinary life, as you all know, if we are convinced that something is true we cannot throw it out and believe its opposite any more. This is especially true of spiritual truth; it has a way of becoming an integral part of your own self, so that you are compelled to dwell upon it and behave according to it, and by such contemplation you find you arrive at a profound condition which has been called the condition of *dhyāna*, or meditation. Through this meditation you have the experience of the ultimate Reality, the spiritual Reality, face to face. This one Being, this grand Divine Identity which is taught by monistic Vedanta, then becomes actually the object of your experience—or the *subject* of your experience, because in that experience you yourself are that Identity. It is at once subject and object, and when you realize it you become transformed.

Mind, it is not merely that you believe in this Identity; you have literally become a different

person. In India, it has been usual to call such a
person *mahāpuruṣa*—great soul or super-man.
Mahā means great and *puruṣa* means soul or
man, but "great man" does not convey in English the sense which is conveyed by the Sanskrit
word *mahāpuruṣa*. The idea is that the limitations of the man—the qualities that confined
him and made him small—have gone. He no
longer has any doubts, he has grasped reality at
its purest, he has found himself; he has become
pure and he has, above all, transcended the limits of time and space and become established in
the eternal truth. That is what makes him a
great soul: he is no longer bound by his body and
its demands. Yes, he also would feel hunger, he
also would feel the need of sleep; but if he didn't
have food and the body were to waste away, it
would not matter to him. That would be the
difference between him and an ordinary man.
Whether he is honored or not honored doesn't
matter in the least to him. If the whole world
were to disappear this moment, it would not
make the slightest difference to him. We are so
frightened by the thought that an H-bomb might
fall somewhere and convert thousands and
thousands of human beings to smithereens. To
such a person it would not make the slighest
difference if his body were to be reduced to invisible dust, because he knows he is not the body.
That which is important to us is nonexistent to

him. So it has been said, ''That which is night to the common man is day to the man of self-control, and that which is day to the common man is night to the man of Self-realization.''[1] Everything becomes entirely different. That is the best that can come to anyone—and everyone will one day realize that state.

2

Some of you may think that monism is one-sided; you may think of it as the path of *jñāna*, or of knowledge, and ask how it can be made applicable to a person who is emotional in nature and prefers to follow the path of devotion. I would contend that while in its philosophical presentation monism does indeed lean heavily on reason and while it is quite natural that some people should follow the path of *jñāna*, monistic Vedanta does not necessarily interpret the ideal in terms of reason, nor must its goal be realized only through the process of reason. It can be realized through any spiritual process; I shall mention two others: the process of devotion, and the process of action.

In supreme love there is also the realization of Divine Identity, and even before that state is realized, it is quite conceivable that one might feel the presence of that same Divinity, the object of our highest love, existing in everyone.

Who can deny that one of the characteristics of love is that it obliterates distinctions and differences and separations? As a matter of fact it might be said that the path of love is best and the path of reason only second best for realizing the monistic ideal, although I must admit that the traditional belief has been just the opposite. Traditionally, it has been said that if you have the sense of unity, of the one Reality in all, you cannot really cultivate devotion, the idea being that devotion can be cultivated only with the sense of duality as ultimate. These have been the traditional conclusions about monistic Vedanta, but we Vedantists who are followers of Sri Ramakrishna and Swami Vivekananda do not accept that view; on the basis of their experience and their teachings we hold that the truth of monism may be practiced and also realized through either mode equally.

The path of devotion is, of course, the path of emotion, and you may say that emotion is not dependable. We all know that emotion can get out of hand. Everybody dislikes being "emotional," and yet it is also well known that emotion is more central to a person than reason. How do you resolve this contradiction? You resolve it by recognizing that emotion can be purified. Then, even if it becomes exceedingly intense, it is a desirable thing; it does not get out of control, it does not betray you or lead you astray.

It is only impure emotion that does so. Nor is it true that reason is always trustworthy. The reasoning of a fanatic sometimes becomes destructive to himself and to his fellow beings. He has his "reasons" and he thinks they are very correct; yet we know they are not. Emotion may betray us; yes, if emotion is impure then it is deadly, but it can be purified and then it is not. Unfortunately, very little attention has been given to the training of emotions and a great deal of attention has been given to the training of reason. But as a seeker of truth you are supposed to have purified your emotions to a great extent before you even begin, and further purification takes place as you practice. It then becomes possible to follow feeling without fear.

Then there is the path of power, or of action. It is not generally recognized, or not as well recognized as it should be, that action is also a very effective way of attaining to the monistic ideal. It is through action that we come in contact with reality, that we know reality, and therefore, you see, the path of action can be a very adequate means of realizing the same truth. You just choose your path according to your own nature.

I have mentioned my views on devotion and action as paths to monistic awareness because in the West, and I may say even in India, when a person says that his ideal is monism, or his philosophy is monism, there is generally this

response, "Oh, he is a dry person; he goes on all
the time analyzing and reasoning." Yes, I sometimes think that monism has suffered because in
trying to present itself it has always used such
dry logical language. But then I don't think there
is any other way of presenting it; even the
dualists, when they try to put their religion in
philosophical form, have had to use dry logical
language. It is really a weakness or a deficiency
in human nature, or in the human situation: we
cannot present anything very clearly to another
person unless we use the language of reason. But
you must remember that the quest for truth is an
individual quest. In school you may receive help
from many people and may yourself help others;
yet each has to know for himself and to understand for himself. In this quest too, in the quest
for ultimate truth, it is an individual matter. If I
do not have any responsibility for making my
experiences and my conclusions intelligible to
you, then I am freed from the necessity of being
logical. If I have only myself to consider, the
language of emotion would do just as well as that
of reason. There is really no justification for
thinking that a person whose ideal is monism is
a dry person. As a matter of fact, the original
books of Vedanta, the Upanishads, which are
essentially monistic, are also highly poetic, so
much so that their composers called themselves
kavi—poet. But the commentators explained

the word as meaning "scholar"; they had to prove that these sages were philosophers, because if they were only poets, then, of course, you might wonder whether you should take their words seriously. Poets you enjoy, but you rarely take a poet's words seriously. But these poets *were* to be taken seriously. They called themselves poets because they had come upon a world of infinite beauty, the world of Brahman or God, and they tried to express it in language that was beautiful too. A language that is highly poetic and at the same time literal, that is the beauty of the Upanishads. So, you see, you can follow the path of reason without being dry. In fact, the path of reason is also a path of devotion. Yes, a person who is seeking truth by means of reason is also a very devoted person. There is a great earnestness in him; he has an ideal for which he will give up everything. So the word *devotion* could be used here also, and in that case the path of reason is another form of the path of love.

I should mention here, however, that whatever your nature or path, it has been found that the monistic approach to truth is not possible except from a standpoint made strong by great moral discipline. That should be understood. But once morally strong, strong through self-discipline, a person may follow whatever path is suited to his own nature, and if he aims at this truth, the one eternal Divinity, he will realize it.

3

These are the general principles of Vedanta philosophy and religion that have appealed to me. I need hardly say that monism, or monistic Vedanta, has not become my philosophy merely officially. I have known Vedantists who say that monistic Vedanta is their philosophy because it provides the philosophic justification of their own spiritual ideal—although that ideal is not itself monistic. Their ideal, for example, may be qualified monism, the highest form of theism. The principal view of qualified monism is that there is only one Reality, containing within itself many distinctions; these distinctions are permanent, eternal distinctions, but the entity containing them is one. In contrast, pure monism will say that *all* distinctions are the result of our ignorance; they actually do not exist. When we imagine their existence we so imagine under the power of ignorance; in reality there is just one indefinable Being in whom there is no division and no distinction, ever.

Nowadays many have found philosophical difficulty in sustaining the thesis of qualified monism and so have been persuaded that, although they are in practice dualistic or theistic, they must adopt the philosophy of monism. Since monism satisfies the demands of reason better than qualified monism, they will admit that monism is the highest ideal, but only as the very "last word." If you ask them, "Aren't *you* going to reach that highest state?" they say, "Not necessarily." For they hold that the state of salvation, or liberation, does not necessarily involve becoming completely identified with Divinity.

There have, in fact, been great Vedantic teachers who have maintained that even in the ultimate there will remain certain permanent distinctions. For example, Sri Ramakrishna used to give this illustration: when the cold wind blows, the water of the sea, which is formless, becomes congealed, frozen into ice; that which was formless takes form. But when the sun rises again, the ice melts away; that which had form becomes formless. Similarly, the cool air of devotion makes the formless Divinity take form, but when the sun of monism rises, then the formed becomes formless. Having said that, he used to add, "But there is a place where the ice never melts. Eternal ice is there, eternal forms of God." Well, some will quote this and say, "Yes, even in the highest realization of Divinity there can be form, and so, although from a logical point of view monism is most satisfying, from a religious point of view I am not a monist." Or another will say, "Yes, I admit that the monistic realization is the last state that comes to the soul; but you do not realize it by your own efforts—it comes of itself; and, anyhow, you cannot realize it until you have gone through all the other stages. So, for practical purposes you might as well forget monism except when you have to discuss philosophy."

You see, there are these different views, and some of you may share them. But I have not found that I have to accept monism in such a limited sense. I have found that monism satisfies me from the standpoint of philosophy and from the standpoint of religion as well. And I have found that as a philosophy it must be true *now*—not just as the "last word." In fact, I have always thought that even as applied to our present state dualistic philosophies, however intricate their arguments, are just the beginning of philosophy. I would not even dignify them by the name "philosophical systems." Indeed, to be more precise, I would say it is qualified monism that is the very beginning of philosophy. Real philosophy comes only when you enter into the realm of monistic thought. It is all very easy and natural to regard what is given to your unillumined mind as the pattern of truth, even of the ultimate truth. That is what all the nonmonistic systems do: they take what they find now, they rub it a little here, polish it a little there and call it a "system of philosophy." That cannot be a system of philosophy, because it is well known that our problem, in ignorance, is not so much a lack in the quantity of our knowledge as in its *quality*. Of course, there are many things to know and we are continually adding to our knowledge, but the quality of our knowledge is not altered by such additions: it is the same in me, an ignorant person, as in the greatest philosopher or the greatest scientist. We all of us take this world to be real, and we try to analyze it, synthesize it, and thereby get some meaning out of it. Our 'I' is not changed, it is still the same base metal. Yes, some of us have got a little better polish on top, but if you scratch that top, there is the same lead underneath.

I would not call any position "philosophy" if it fails to recognize that it is my present state of being and of knowing that is the source of all the trouble. In my present state I am not able to make peace with myself. I am continually torn and divided within myself; the claims of the body encroach upon the claims of the Spirit, and the claims of the mind want to ignore the claims of the body as well as those of the Spirit, and, of course, the Spirit will ignore the claims of both body and mind. Until we have really established ourselves on our highest level, which is that of the Spirit, there is a continuous loss of equilibrium; we are continually moving and never able to attain any stability of being. We all know this to be true. That is the real problem of any individual seeker of truth. If you want to write a book on philosophy or give lectures on philosophy or persuade others, then there are many things you must do—whether they are worth doing, I doubt—but, whatever you do, you must first make peace within yourself.

In Indian philosophy, in Vedanta particularly, there have been two approaches to reality. Most of the religions of the world have sought after God. The traditional religious approach everywhere has been theistic; this is particularly true of the Semitic religions. Find God, find God; He is the explanation; He is the creator of the universe; it is He who has become this world; He is the proof, and so on. This approach is called in Sanskrit *brahmajñāna*, knowledge of Brahman. Through it one may arrive at a dualistic conception of God in relation to the souls, or at a qualified monistic conception—or, if you go far enough, at absolute monism.

But there has also been another approach, which is called *ātmajñāna*, knowledge of the Self. In Sanskrit there is this injunction, "*Ātmānam viddhi*" — "Know the Self" or "Know thy Self." It is said that if we could understand our own self we would have the key to the whole universe. In this approach a true philosopher starts with self-knowledge, with inquiry into himself. I have many times drawn your attention to this fact, that your universe is really a part of yourself. Although you might think that you are a part of the universe and not the universe a part of you, a little thinking—and that is rightly called philosophical thinking in that it differs from instinctive thinking—a little real thinking makes you realize that the universe is part of yourself. How do you know this universe exists? That this universe exists you know only in your own consciousness. You cannot get away from this fact, ever.

I have often thought that the life of philosophy begins when you suddenly start to feel that this universe which you instinctively think is extended outside yourself—and of which you think yourself a minute part—is in reality part of your own self-existence. Yes, it is in me that the universe appears real, in my consciousness. And if consciousness is not *my* consciousness, then it cannot be consciousness at all. There cannot be any consciousness except self-consciousness; for wherever there is consciousness, the sense of the self is pervasive with it. In fact, consciousness *is* self-consciousness.

Think about it: you cannot say "the tree exists"; all you can truly say is "I perceive that the tree exists," "I know that the tree exists." To be sure, in order to abbreviate your language you do not go through this rigmarole of saying "I know this, I know this, I know this." It would be unbearable if every sentence had to begin with "I perceive" or "I know"; yet you would be wrong if you forgot in your thinking that whatever you know is contained in consciousness—in your *Ātman* or Self. Consciousness is not contained within the body, the body is contained within consciousness. The recognition "I have a body," that is also in my consciousness.

My friends, once you begin to think in these terms, you will be surprised to find what wonderful freedom comes to you. Nor is that all. You will find that you have come to closer grips with *this* world's reality. You have become more effective; your eyes have become clearer; you understand things better; if truth is your goal, you have a greater chance of attaining that truth. Then you will no longer have any doubt that it is a more effective way of looking at reality. And once you start thinking of all reality in this way, as existing only in your own consciousness, you cannot but end up by accepting monism as the truth, now.

I must say that this second approach, this knowledge of the Self, has not been so popular an approach in religion as knowledge of Brahman or God. And this is, I think, in some ways too bad. For the *ātmajñāna* approach, as I have just indicated, forces you to recognize that monism is not only the "last word" in religion, it is the first

word as well. It is the only truth, whether for
theory or for practice, in philosophy or religion,
both now and always.

However, I find myself that I like both these
approaches — *brahmajñāna* and *ātmajñāna.*
You will excuse this "I" and "mine," won't you?
Since you have come to listen to "A View of
Vedanta," you will have to bear with me when I
become personal. Yet I think such an account
may prove profitable to you, at least in this
respect—you will come to see that Vedanta is
not something which everyone is expected to
accept in the same way. Some may accept one
approach, others another, and some few may
like all of them. I have found that students of
Vedanta sometimes become disconsolate because certain ideas expressed in Vedanta do not
appeal to them. I have assured them that they
need not feel uncomfortable on this account. As
I said earlier, it is not expected that each person
appreciate, or accept, all the things that are contained in this vast system of thought. A person
goes to a store, finds many different models of
suits, but is not expected to buy all of them, only
the ones that appeal to him. Vedanta is that kind
of system; a very comprehensive system of
thought and of religion, and you accept only
what you can.

For myself, as I say, I have found that I really
like all approaches. The devotional approach

does not bother me. In fact, I really have liked the practice of devotion very much. Nor have I found any conflict between the devotional and rational approaches.

4

How I arrived at this state I myself have pondered. I am not really what you would call a philosopher; in fact, I have never liked philosophy as such. When I went to college I used to escape from the philosophy classes, as a general rule. I rarely attended because I didn't like the discourses of our professor of philosophy. I found that those profound truths, which are in actuality so elusive, were reduced by such professors to matter-of-fact terms and then reeled out of their notebooks, or off their lips from memory, and the superficiality of the whole thing used to nauseate me; at the very beginning of the hour I would leave the class. The net result is that I have never become a philosopher or even a proper student of philosophy.

This is what always used to irk me: it is true that there is no escaping the use of logical language in the presentation of truth, but you can overdo it; you can get into a condition in which you think that logical manipulation is philosophy, forgetting that it is really not philosophy at all. The first concern of a real philosopher, or of a student of philosophy, should be to learn how to approach reality at its freshest, in its native state. What is the reality of your own being? What is the reality of a flower, of a tree, of a cow, of a man? If you reduce it to a term, you have already killed it. "The letter killeth." Yes, the moment you reduce a living experience to a word, it becomes an idea, a concept in your mind, and it is dead. It is as if you had drawn a map, or a line drawing, of a beautiful scene. You may with your ink show the contours, or even the trees and such things, but would you say that this presents the *reality* of that scene? Would you consider it the same as that beautiful scene? No. But philosophers do just that; they forget that their philosophies are only line drawings of the living reality. It was this that used to irk me; you cannot sacrifice the living reality if you are to find truth.

I do not deny that philosophy calls for precision. You must go to the living reality, but what about the state of mind you take with you? You may go there with a mind that is very diffuse, very uncertain. Knowledge calls for certainty; it cannot permit any kind of vagueness or confusion of mind, for that is the equivalent of ignorance multiplied many times. I believe that reality can be approached and reflected in the mind in its entire beauty, its entire spontaneity. Spontaneity is not the same thing as vagueness;

it is possible to have spontaneity, the living quality, and to have great clarity as well. But I admit that to achieve this requires a special discipline.

As a matter of ideas or concepts only, the philosophic discipline is a discipline of the reason; it is a way of thinking rationally. You have aptitude, let us say, and then you are taught by the study of logic and other disciplines how to think philosophically. But there is another discipline by which the mind is capable of the spontaneous grasp of reality at its freshest, at its very origin. That discipline, I have found, calls for self-abnegation. By self-abnegation I mean relinquishment of what you know to be only superficial and therefore untrue, of what you know to be a veil covering the face of truth. You not only have to reject this in your thought, you have to reject it in your behavior, for in our present state thought is only a pale reflection of behavior. I do not, for example, see how a seeker of truth—a true student of philosophy—can be all involved with this world, going here and going there, enjoying the so-called good things of life, and at the same time reflect in his own mind reality as it is. I do not see how he can grasp reality fully and understand what it is. I just cannot see it. You may say, "If a philosophy student behaved as you require, he would be antisocial; what kind of life is this for a student of philosophy?" My friends, even if you want to gain a little something of this world you will find you cannot distract yourself; you have to give your full attention to it. And here you are trying to capture the heart of reality and you do not think it calls for your full attention! I say it does call for your full attention; your full mind and your full heart have to be given to it.

Well, through the grace of God, through chance, or through natural development, I have always felt from my early days as if I did not belong to this earth. There was always within me this haunting sense of not belonging, and that was a great help. I was not caught in the whirlpool of things of which the whole human society is made up. These things, so important to many, did not convey much meaning to me; they appeared to be just self-indulgence and dissipation of valuable energy. So when the desire to find truth came with great force in my life, I was able very easily to withdraw my mind; because, you see, I had not been caught. I came very soon to the conclusion that since the body is mortal it could not be the truth. I do not think this idea came because of any reasoning but rather presented itself as an obvious fact. The body could not be the truth about myself, and, therefore, it could not be the truth about anyone else. If I were to think that the person to whom I talked was only a bundle of flesh, I would not talk with him. What is the use of talking to a corpse? But human beings, fortunately, are not matter; no being is; not even so-called matter is matter, fortunately. And I was able to see that this universe is really a great mask over the face of the ultimate truth. Forms are continually hiding the reality, but I was fortunate enough to catch glimpses of this reality behind the mask of things, and I became, therefore, an ardent devotee of this truth.

5

I remember I was then in high school, and I wanted to read that great book of Swami Vivekananda's called *Jnana-Yoga*. It is not a book written by him, but a number of his lectures on similar subjects brought together and published under this title. It is a most extraordinary collection. I was able to borrow that book from one of the teachers. At first he would not give it to me; he thought that it was too abstruse for me, that I wasn't ready for it. But I begged him to lend it to me, and when he finally did I found it deeply moving. I used to shed copious tears on the pages of that book. On every page is the truth that everything is really the Spirit, the one Spirit, which is the very essence of all perfection, that Spirit which we ourselves are and for which we have been restless for ages and ages—some knowing, most of us not knowing, but restless, all of us, for that vision. You see, the description of it was so vivid that it could not but move me. It was from reading *Jnana-Yoga* that I became a convert, if such a word can be used, to Vedantic monism. That monism, as it is taught by Swami Vivekananda, is not a partial presentation of truth; it subsumes all the truths of the Spirit, even those spoken of by the theists.

From reading *Jnana-Yoga* I came to certain conclusions and although none of them were new conclusions, they meant a great deal to me and they became, as it were, part of my own philosophy. These truths that appealed to me were gradually integrated into a sort of system in my own mind. In this system, I recognized that the instinctive sense that there exist different individual beings and different kinds of beings was false, that these "differences" were the product of my own false existence—that is to say, of my own identification with the body— that my true existence and my true self was Spirit only, and finally that the Spirit in every thing is the same Spirit.

One further conclusion I came to is a little unusual. There is, you know, in Vedanta one commonly accepted way of understanding the variety of things we see here. In this understanding it is held that there is the same Spirit everywhere, but in some it is more manifest, in others less manifest. For example, in animals it is less manifest, in man it is more manifest; in a good man it is more manifest than in an evil man, and in a saint it is most manifest. All of us ordinarily recognize these degrees in the manifestation of the Spirit. But I came to the conclusion that such differentiation of degrees is another of the false conclusions of our own ignorant state of existence. There are no degrees of manifestation, more here and less there; there is equal manifestation of the same Divine Spirit everywhere. In the living, in the nonliving, in the saint and in the sinner, the Divine Spirit is fully and therefore equally manifested.

You may say this violates our experience; we have to recognize that there are different species of beings. Do I mean to say that we ought to ignore all these differences or that I don't feel called upon to explain them? No, I recognize these differences, but I do not agree with your interpretation of them, that is all. Provided that you admit the whole universe is a self-manifestation of the Divine, then I would accept differences in that manifestation; at least when I am not caught up too high in monistic awareness I would. For it is also one of the conclusions of Vedanta that, although there is an unutterable and indefinable Identity that is the ultimate truth—or that is *the* truth—still, if you dwell on the relative plane, you will see differences.

Whatever explanations you give of it, in experience you will see the world of differences. But you need not interpret these differences in the way you do when ignorant.

I have always felt that there are infinite differences because self-manifestation depends on difference, but that, however different in form, all beings are equally valuable as manifestations of the Spirit. Each species, as it were, represents a different kind of self-manifestation of the Divine, in no way inferior or superior to any other kind. We human beings, for example, interpret the rest of the known universe or even the imagined universe, in terms of human consciousness. So if we see in trees, say, very little of human consciousness or behavior according to human consciousness, then we think that trees are vastly inferior to human beings in the scale of things. But that is a mistake. Why should you think that all manifestations are in terms of human consciousness and human behavior? To think so means that you are equating humanity with Divinity; but humanity is not Divinity. A human being, when he realizes God, transcends the limitations and peculiarities of human nature.

So I came to the conclusion that everything that is, is equally divine. Later I came upon a verse, first as quoted from the *Bhagavad-Gita* in a lecture of Swami Vivekananda and then afterwards in the *Bhagavad-Gita* itself. That verse

speaks of "everywhere the same Divinity existing in the same way." And it is further said in the
same verse, "He who sees Divinity so existing
reaches thereby the highest condition."[2] Just
notice these terms. It does not say that everywhere God exists but not in the same degree. It
says "same"—God existing in the same manner,
in the same degree, in everything: in the tree, in
the dog, in the saint, in the sinner, everywhere
the same. Another verse in the *Gita* says the
illumined soul sees the same Being in a dog, in a
cow, in a learned brahmin, in a low-caste person,
in an untouchable;[3] he sees the same God,
equally, everywhere. Yes, this is it, the truth of
which I spoke; this truth *has* been recognized.
But I have not found that this phase of Vedanta is
much emphasized, even in monism. Those who
follow monism, even they will make distinctions. If you ask them, "Do you think God is
equally manifest in a cow and in a saint?" they
will at once protest, "Oh, no, no, no," and they
will launch into an elaborate explanation of how
ignorance is thicker in the dog than in the scholar, of how this thickness has come into existence and how it becomes thinner; then they
will bring in the *gunas—tamas* and *rajas* and
sattva—saying that the dog has more of *tamas*
and the brahmin more of *sattva* and, therefore,
this, that, and the other thing. I will accept that
view, but only as a second-best view. Sometimes

we don't like to remain on such a high plane of thought; we like to come down to a lower plane and find a little comfort. Well, as such, I shall accept it, but I shall also know that it is only for the sake of comfort, not for the sake of truth. If I am to be true, then I shall perch in a less comfortable position, and there I find that all these *gunas* and so on are just our own distinctions. It is because I want a world of order for myself that I say here God is more manifest, there He is less manifest, and so on.

I became convinced, and I have found it hard to shake off this conviction, that the same God is equally existent in all. I came to the further conclusion that the very idea that God is manifest is itself false. There is no question of manifestation; God just is, that is all. It is not that God is first transcendental and absolute and then manifests as this universe. All such ideas are false. I came to the conclusion that there is this one Brahman, this one Divine Reality, that I am one with it, and that what prevents my experiencing this truth is my own wrong thinking—thinking, for example, that there is no ultimate, or else thinking that there is an ultimate but there is a penultimate also, and so on. Such thinking, it seems to me, is at the root of the trouble. And so I say simply this: I cannot perceive this truth because there is something wrong with this which I call my mind.

If I see this world of different men, animals, and so on, it's because I am functioning through the mind, the senses, and the body. If you ask me, "Well, how do you explain the existence of your own mind, senses, and body?" I answer, I don't have to explain them. That I am a sick person, a spiritually sick person, is admitted; otherwise why should I not see the truth? Why should there be any obstructions? Knowing I am sick, I shall recognize the conditions of my present perception as part of my sickness. My problem is to get rid of this sickness. If this body, mind, and senses still remain after I have recovered, then I shall seek an explanation of them. If in a delirium I think that my nose has turned into the trunk of an elephant, do I have to answer the question, "How did I come to have a long nose?" No, when I recover I will know that it was all delirium, that there was no trunk there at all. And if I have mostly recovered from my delirium but have not completely lost the sense that I have an elephant's trunk, then, since I have recovered a little sanity, I will tell myself the trunk is part of my illness, nothing is really wrong with my nose. So I don't have to explain those things that are part of the illness itself. No, what I have to do is to get rid of the illness, to recover quickly. It is I who have endowed you, who are God Himself, with minds and bodies and peculiar behavior of various kinds; it is I

who have created this universe from the highest
state of consciousness down to the total lack of
consciousness; it is I who have projected my
body, mind, and senses. All these things are my
projections, and, therefore, my constant effort is
to undo this mischief in myself. When that is
done, the whole problem of philosophy will be
solved for me.

6

You see, to me everything in this universe is
real; there is nothing which is unreal except the
form and the name—the ideas that I have held
about reality in my own mind. So having found
the source of all troubles within my own mind, I
am quite content to think that that is where all
checking and correction should be made. My
own personal experience has confirmed me in
that conclusion. I found that when I could bring
about change within myself, the whole universe
changed. From that experience I evolved a sort of
formula. But, mind that, I am saying nothing
new; you will find it all in Vedanta. If I can claim
a little novelty it is only that I may have put
things in a little different way; probably they
have not been stated in exactly that way in the
books. For example, it is said in the books that a
scattered mind is not fit for the realization of
spiritual truth, that you have to have concentra-

tion. What I have found is an interrelatedness between the mind and the reality it apprehends. When the mind is scattered, it is also limited and gross and much mixed up with the body; in such a state when you look outward you find the universe is also essentially gross and broken up into an infinite number of forms of different kinds. Consciousness itself, both within oneself and outside in the selves of others, is perceived as essentially physical. As regards God, to such a mind He is almost nonexistent. I have found that these three things—the mind, the world, and God—are related to one another as aspects of one thing. If you can bring about a change in any one of the elements of this complex, you will find the others change too. If you make a practice of thinking that there are no gross beings in this universe, that they are spiritual beings with only an appearance of grossness, you will find your mind has become quieted, less scattered and less gross, you will find yourself to be essentially a spiritual being, and the presence of God will not seem so far off. Or if you can think that God is everywhere and very close to you, then you will find your idea of yourself, your idea of the universe, and your state of mind will all undergo simultaneous change. Finally, if by direct means you can purify, and quiet your mind, then your world, your idea of yourself, and your awareness of God will change correspondingly.

I find this formula applies all the way. The
more concentrated and quieted the mind becomes, the finer it becomes and the finer this
universe appears to be. A time comes when your
mind attains to a great state of calmness and
becomes very fine in its nature; the whole universe then seems to have come together into one
entity with the thread of divine presence passing
through all the forms, just as it says in the
Bhagavad-Gita.[4] You find that God comes so
close to you that He saturates everything,
everywhere, like the insinuating presence of a
perfume. And as regards yourself, you no longer
feel identified with the body and the mind. The
sense of time and space begins to dissolve away.
You walk ten miles and it seems as if you have
walked only half a mile. Time passes and you do
not recognize that many hours have gone. Similarly, the things you do no longer have the same
tiring effect. Altogether you find the tempo of
the universe has changed for you completely.
For good it has changed. Night and day, the passing of the seasons, the conditions of the
weather—none of these have the same effect on
you at all. You are no longer tied down to
changes in the outside world.

All these things prove to me first of all, as I
have said, the interrelatedness of the state of
mind with what is revealed to it as real. And
second, that there are various levels of one's

existence—which is only to say a little more emphatically what I have said all along. Consider for example the various levels on which one may exist in relation to God. Suppose you are in a state of mind where the sense of distinction remains; your mind has become very fine but it has not yet lost itself. Then if you have experience of God, it will be the highest theistic experience; you may see forms of God, there on that level of existence; you may feel intense devotion towards Him, and you will enjoy all the other experiences that go with devotion. You will like to call God Father or Mother, Friend or Lord; you will feel like prostrating yourself at His feet, giving your whole being away in His service, just to please Him. All those things which are indicated in the books of devotion and exemplified in the lives of great saints and sages will become manifest in you. Then suppose you come down from that high state to a lower state. There you will find that God is no longer so close to you, no longer do you feel that intense devotion.

In other words, here is a study of your own being, not your true being, but this associated being made up of mind, life, senses, and body. You notice that as changes take place in that complex, the nature of your experiences changes and the reality revealed to it changes. And as you begin to experience different revelations, you become further confirmed in the view that the secret of all the problems of philosophy and religion lies in your own being. Never—never for a moment—will you find fault with anything else.

Yes, there is still the problem of how I became endowed with this body and mind, but as I have already explained, this is the answer that I have given to myself: now I am sick and so cannot explain these things. I shall become well and then, if they persist, I shall explain them. Of course, you could still ask, "Getting sick and recovering from that sickness, doesn't that require to be explained?" No, it doesn't. Such is the nature of that recovery that you will forget you were ever sick; so there will not be any need, or even any possibility, of explaining that sickness. That is the peculiarity of it. Time itself goes, and therefore circumstances cannot be remembered. Remembrance is in time, you see; remembrance is of things that have happened in time, and since time itself goes away, there can be no problem remembered and no problem to solve. You may say, "Well, that is a very peculiar situation." If, in this ignorant state, you want to call it peculiar, by all means do so; but remember that you would not call it peculiar in the state of recovery, because there is nothing, no object at all, to think about there. Just you are, and that is perfection.

I must tell you that when practicing this

monism I found that my mind would undergo sudden revulsions. When you have been long accustomed to one way of thinking and are teaching the mind to think very differently, it doesn't hold on to the new thought easily. Suddenly, like the movement of a strong instinct, the mind will go back to its original way of thinking, and when it does, it has a tendency of creating doubts about whether you were right in thinking the new way. To think that the whole universe as you have known it for years and years—and if you believe in reincarnation, for ages and ages, for millions of births—to think that the whole scheme was wrong, that is not easy. Sometimes my mind would raise doubts of this kind, but I would remind myself that although I might have thought one way for ages and ages, that had not answered the fundamental questions of life; therefore, I would say to my mind, let us not go back to the same old way of thinking. I would reason that the old way had proved itself inadequate, and besides in the new way of thinking wide vistas opened up before me, vistas undreamt of in the old way. Here I found that everything was cramped and closed; but there, in the new way of thinking, I found everything wide open, there was no end to how far one could go, thinking in this new way. And so I would persuade myself not to go back to the old way, but to hold on to this new way. Such an

effort to persuade the mind to retain the monistic outlook is itself a kind of spiritual practice.

7

So you can see that when it came to religion, I
did not find that I had to reject anything in Vedanta. I have practiced ritualism and found it
quite satisfying. I have practiced meditation and
found it quite satisfying. I have absorbed myself
in devotional attitudes; I have found that, too,
quite satisfying. I have also practiced the path of
jñāna, or reasoning, a great deal and I have found
that, also, quite satisfying. I have become absorbed in action, and I have found that satisfying
too. In other words, from my own personal experience I have been convinced that all paths are
equally fruitful, for all equally spell for me the
same truth, the same monism. I have not, therefore, seen any contradiction in following a variety of paths.

Yes, this is the great game. Something is there
because of which the one reality appears as manifold. But I am not convinced that the individuals in this manifold differ in the quality of Divinity that they manifest. In this, all are the same.
There are differences, but they are differences of
kind only. For example, there is a kind of consciousness, let us say tree consciousness, which
is different from human consciousness, but it is

equally effective, equally great. I can imagine also, along the same train of thought, that there is a kind of consciousness known as stone consciousness which is equally as important, as significant, and as high as human consciousness or as angelic consciousness—it is just different in kind. As long as I am completely identified with human consciousness, I shall never understand stone consciousness or tree consciousness or lion consciousness, but if I could become pure consciousness, separating myself from the human ingredients in me, I could then identify myself with any type of consciousness and perceive it intuitively, directly. I myself have known some who have done that, and they say that tree consciousness, for instance, is an equally high state of consciousness, but completely different from human consciousness. It is so different that when the hour passed in which their consciousness was beyond the limits of its own kind of knowing and they had identified once more with human consciousness, they could not express what they had experienced in that state of elevation in terms of their human existence.

Yes, everything is God and not less than God, anywhere. Everything is Brahman, everything is Spirit. If you realize this and live up to it, you can sometimes pour yourself out in actions and in service, and you can sometimes pour yourself in, in contemplation of this ever-existent, infinitely existing, all-pervasive Spirit. That is all there is to it.

1. *Bhagavad-Gita,* 2.69.
2. Ibid., 13.28.
3. Ibid., 5.18.
4. Ibid., 7.7.

A VIEW OF VEDANTA — II

1

I AM SURE most of you know that Vedanta is both a religion and a philosophy. In India it has been very difficult to keep philosophy apart from religion, because it was accepted from very ancient times that there are realities other than those we can perceive with our senses or infer with our intellect, and since philosophy is nothing but man's effort to harmonize all the facts of experience, we are absolutely obligated to take all revelations of reality—the invisible as well as the visible—into consideration. In order to have a true philosophy we must, then, be capable of experiences that go beyond those of ordinary men. And you cannot have those experiences unless you have undergone some religious training, some form of worship or contemplation or meditation. So you see how religion had to become mixed up with philosophy, particularly when that philosophy is of the status of Vedanta. We are satisfied with this situation; indeed, we think we are quite right in not separating religion from philosophy or philosophy from religion.

In this talk I would like to present to you what I myself have thought about philosophy and its problems and, on the basis of my conception of philosophy, to present to you also what I have thought religion should be.

I have always been a little reluctant to study philosophy as such. And if you ask me how I dare, then, to stand before you and speak on philosophical subjects, I should tell you this: although I don't like the study of academic philosophy, I have always found myself asking questions about those ultimate problems with which every system of philosophy is concerned. You cannot always say why or when your thoughts originate; you cannot always know whether you began to like those thoughts under the influence of certain persons or whether you were just born in the atmosphere of those thoughts—you just don't know. So I won't be able to tell you what ideas I had to start with, as I began to learn to think, but I remember a few things which could be called landmarks in my philosophical life—and, for the matter of that, also in my religious life.

It was while I was in high school that these things began to come into my life—no, I should go further back. I recall a very memorable event. There was a gentleman living in Bengal, an extraordinary person he was. He had the blessedness of having met Sri Ramakrishna and of having talked with him and also with Swami Vivekananda. Sri Ramakrishna had made this gentleman very welcome, and he turned out to be a great man indeed. He was great in many respects, not only in his religious life but also as a nationalist and an educationist. His name was Aswini Kumar Dutta. In those days we used to hear of his college, in a small town in Bengal, where both the students and the teachers were exemplary. Anybody fortunate enough to study in that college was envied by us. Now, Mr. Dutta was a very ardent devotee, and he at one time gave a series of lectures which were afterwards brought out by a sort of disciple of his under the name *Bhakti-Yoga.* That book was written in Bengali and has been translated into English. Even now from time to time I take this book from the shelf and read it, and I am profoundly stimulated by it.

It was when I was in junior high school that I first came upon this book. A neighbor had procured it and read to me a certain poem from it. It impressed me very deeply. So I begged him to lend the book to me, and some time after he did. And when I finished reading that book it was as though a great storm had blown through my life. I was literally turned topsy-turvy—everything completely changed. The whole world looked entirely different to me; the whole purpose of life changed. I may say that it was a very unusual experience and a real turning point in my life. I remember how dispassionate I felt, as if I was the spectator of this world we see. It lasted for some months: nothing used to bother me, nothing used to affect me, I felt deeply peaceful.

There came afterwards a period in which I no longer was so conscious about all these metaphysical things. But later, when I was in high school, one day a friend of mine and I were discussing the problem of immortality—of all things! Our mathematics teacher had come into the classroom to give us our lesson, but we hadn't noticed him. He asked, "Are you interested in these things?" We begged his forgiveness. Then he said, "If you are interested, see me after school hours." That again was something every important in my life, because the teacher was a follower of Sri Ramakrishna and Swami Vivekananda. He said he would be very glad to hold a class for us every Sunday morning; if we wanted, we could come and bring our friends. As it happened, only three of us came, and afterwards only two remained. He started with the Upanishads, but we did not take to them. The Upanishadic sayings are such straight statements; you are not asked to argue or reason; the truths are just baldly put before you. We could not get our teeth into them, and after two or three classes we told him that they just didn't seem to affect us. So then he took up a book of Swami Vivekananda's.

Most of Swami Vivekananda's published works, as you know, are lectures that were taken down and put into book form. In those days there was a collection of his lectures called *A Study of*

Religion; I don't know whether it is still being published or not. Well, this teacher took it up, and from the first it caught hold of us and completely absorbed our attention. I remember that the classes were begun in the autumn. Autumn is very beautiful in Bengal. The sky is quite clear, everything seems serene, and the sunlight is pure gold. We used to go very early to this class, and I still remember how I used to look through the windows to the golden morning; and as I listened to this talk—the study of this book— something within me tried to burst out, as if it were trying to come out of a cage where it had long been imprisoned. I felt a great longing to get out—I don't know just what it was I wanted to get out of, but I felt this world to be a sort of limitation, a bondage for me, and something within me wanted to come out of this bondage. I may say that was the true beginning of my philosophical and religious life. I think I was then in the first or second year of high school.

But even before I undertook this study of Swami Vivekananda, I had been very fond of the writings of Rabindranath Tagore. I take this occasion to express my indebtedness to him. When I first came upon them, his books seemed to open an entirely new world before me. I don't think I was sentimental—I was never sentimental—but the beauty and the thought of his poems, and even of his prose writings, used to impress me very deeply. Not only were the language and style in which he wrote extraordinary, but the thoughts he expressed, the subjects he dwelt on—previous writers had not dealt with them. He seemed to go deeper into everything. And after I had read him, whatever I looked at began to reveal to me an unwonted depth; I think that helped me in understanding Swami Vivekananda. The net effect of this study of Rabindranath Tagore was that I felt a great longing for something which was not of this earth. Tagore oftentimes spoke of the far-off. He used to call God "the Far-off"—he would say, "I am athirst for the Far-off." And my heart, also, would be filled with longing for something which was afar and yet very real. Then I came to the study of Swami Vivekananda, as I was telling you, and a great restlessness seized me. And when it seized me, my mind began to think about its meaning.

I may say here that this study of Swami Vivekananda—of his lectures and of his life— was highly satisfactory to me. It deepened my life and made me really thoughtful. In those days I used to envy this friend of mine who joined me in that study because he was able to think original thoughts, whereas I didn't have any original thoughts. I could understand everything that I read or everything that was said—that much I had. But I could not think things out for myself, whereas he could, and I used to envy him. He, too, became a devotee of Sri Ramakrishna. We were together for years and years; we used to spend as many hours together as we could when we were in high school and also when we went to college. We were very close, and so I used to feel a little something lacking in my own thoughtfulness. But it did come, I am happy to say. I began to find new things in the world that I saw; new thoughts arose in my mind. Sometimes these thoughts were such that I would hesitate to speak them out, they were so different from the thoughts we had read about in books or heard other people express. You see, if you think differently from other people, you really do not know whether you are normal; quite possibly there is something wrong with you. But on the other hand there is also a chance that you might be thinking rightly—a little differently it is true, but rightly still.

Now here I must admit that, being under the influence of Swami Vivekananda, I was prejudiced in my choice of philosophy. Of course Swami Vivekananda taught Vedanta, as you all know, and you might say my choice of Vedanta and my satisfaction with that philosophy were due solely to my devotion to him. You might say it was not a product of my thinking, it was just a product of my allegiance. Yes, in a sense that is true. As a matter of fact, even great philosophers

do not start with an empty mind; they start with
what they have imbibed from other people and
from their environment. Real originality comes
afterwards, when a person begins to review all
the problems and all the answers he has learned
and taken for granted and finds other reasons,
other systematizations of these ideas—that is
where the originality of a philosopher or thinker
comes in. I may say this, that I did think about
things. And although there is little that can be
called original in my thought, the emphasis may
well be different, and that would be one justification for my speaking on this subject this
morning.

2

And so I began to think. I really don't know why
this thought came or why it became an important thought with me, but even in those early
days I knew that we cannot have any understanding of anything, we cannot be sure of anything, except through our own consciousness.
Actually, there is nothing else. How do I know
that there is a world? How do I know that there
are other people? We take all these things for
granted. I am sorry to say that even philosophers
have taken these things for granted. In fact, in
Western philosophy you have a tradition of con-
tempt for pure subjectivism; you say it is false

because it ignores the vaster reality of this world and of other people. We don't feel that way in India: there, subjectivism has not been under a cloud.

The more you think about it, the more you will come to the conclusion that you are the axis of everything—no, I would even say that you are the receptacle in which everything is contained. There is nothing beyond yourself. Long, long ago I became convinced of that fact. You will probably laugh at the crudity of my thinking and of my experimentation on this problem. But I used to think like this: when I close my eyes, I do not see any form or any color or any such thing. Do you, any of you? I still think it is a very good, although a very commonplace experiment. I close my eyes—the whole world of forms disappears; I open my eyes—all leaps into knowledge, the world of forms is spread before me. I say that if this world and all this infinite number of men and things were real, then every moment they would assert themselves. You may say, "Oh, no, the things are there, but unless you perceive them you would not *know* that they are there." My view is that if anything is really true, nothing in me should be able to repudiate or nullify it—nothing. Whether I look at it or do not look at it, it will still be real to me, I shall still perceive it. Of course, I know that at once you will reject this sort of idea. You will say, "That's a very

funny way of looking at things. After all, there
may be someone talking near you, but if you are
deaf you will not hear him. It does not mean that
the man is not talking." You see what you are
doing? You see how accustomed you have become to a big error? You are taking for granted, as
the standard of all reality, your present habit of
doing or hearing or perceiving. In our present
limited, ignorant state, unless we have the
cooperation of the senses things do not become
available to us. But if things are real—by which I
mean if they are eternal—why should they wait
upon the cooperation of the senses?

The ordinary universe, you see, is made up of
sense forms—the five sense forms corresponding to the five senses of perception. By the eyes
we see form and color, by the ears we hear sound,
and so on; everything in this world is made up of
these five sense forms. And if I have these
senses, then I recognize these forms; if I don't
have the senses, I don't recognize them. When
you say, "I see a person standing ten feet off,"
what you really mean is, in your consciousness
such a person is standing ten feet off. Whatever
you know, you know in your consciousness; you
do not know it otherwise. You are just like people in a submarine who see outside things
through a periscope. They do not directly see
anything outside the submarine—a boat coming
or anything—they see it indirectly through mir-

rors. The truth is, we also are seeing everything in our consciousness indirectly, through these instruments, the senses; yet what we say is, I am seeing a man, I am seeing a tree, I am seeing this, I am seeing the other thing. In every case, what I see is in me. That is what stuck with me, that conclusion: that everything is really part of my own consciousness.

But thinking in this way had other consequences which were not too happy. If it is true that things—outside things, the so-called world of objects—really are dependent on my senses and that when the senses do not cooperate they do not exist, then probably there is nothing. There may be some reality, an indefinable reality, but certainly not the reality we *think* is existing outside of us. I also felt, by the same token, that I am not sure I am a body. How do I know I am a body? There again the cooperation of the senses is necessary. Mostly it is the sense of touch; also it is the sense of sight. The eyes see parts of the body, but mostly we feel it, through the sense of touch. That touch can be exterior, it can also be interior. So if I come to the conclusion that outside realities are not independent existences—certainly that they don't exist as they appear to us—then I also have to take the same attitude towards this body of mine.

As for the mind, I had long before become convinced that this mind is nothing but a slave

of the body and the senses. It repeats the same
thing the senses perceive and bring home to it; it
does not seem to contribute anything new. Some
philosophers have said there are such things as
innate ideas; that is to say, there are ideas in the
mind which cannot be derived from any sense
perception. But what real evidence is there for
such ideas? If they are there how can you know
them? Can you really know your mind? It
changes constantly; you cannot put your hands
on it and say, "This is the mind." Have you
noted this? With the mind you do all your thinking, everything; but you do not know what the
mind is. It is as though water has been so covered
with foam that you are not able to see it at all. If I
ask you, "Is the water clean? What color is it?"
you cannot tell me. Thoughts so cover the mind
that what the mind is in itself—what ideas there
may be that are innate to it and so forth—we do
not know. So if we forget these innate ideas, the
other ideas in the mind seem to be nothing but
echoes of what the senses have perceived or of
what the senses are trying to do or are craving
for. So I came to the conclusion that not only am
I not this body, I am also not this mind.

Later I read Vedanta philosophy and learned
that Vedantists say that whatever is the object of
knowledge is not yourself. The object cannot be
the subject. If you point out that we all the time
say such things as "I know myself," I would

answer, "That's only a way of speaking." Upon analysis it is found that the knower is not knowable. Whatever is the object of consciousness is not itself consciousness. The mind—in fact, both body and mind—are therefore considered different from that entity, that conscious entity, which we may call the soul.

In the end I became quite confused about these two things: first, everything is true only insofar as it is in my consciousness; and second, not only am I not this body, I am not even this mind. I had, as I have said, been convinced that as an entity in itself, separate from the sense impressions in it, the mind is not real—at least, it cannot be known to be real. But if the mind itself is not real, then what is left? Well, I could not get away from this conclusion either: that there is *something* in this universe—it may not be a bird, it may not be a beast, it may not be a man, it may not be a cow, it may not be anything we perceive through the senses and through the mind, but there must be something—something which creates the stimulus. Otherwise why do you think we would perceive things at all? In whatever way we perceive, there must be something which is stimulating consciousness. So I accepted this view, that there is some reality outside me, as there is some reality inside me. Then my thought proceeded in this way and came to this conclusion: if this body and this

mind, including the senses and everything, are
unreal, then that which is outside, behind all
these sense forms, and that which is within
must be one thing, since there is nothing to
separate my own being from the larger being of
this universe; and if that which is within me,
that is to say, my own true self, is a self-
conscious being, then that which exists outside
must also be a self-conscious being.

3

At that time I came upon *The Science and
Philosophy of Religion,* another collection of
some lectures of Swami Vivekananda. I remember how I then made a determined effort to perceive that reality behind all these sense forms.
This is the way I reasoned: If there is such a
thing, it must be God. Because if it is infinite, if
it is beyond matter and beyond mind, then
whatever name you give it, it is the same thing
as that which theists call God—He who is existent everywhere. And if He is everywhere existing, how is it, and why is it, that I am not able to
perceive Him? I did not accept the view that
while we are as we are, we cannot perceive God;
I just would not accept that. I said to myself, if
everything is really this divine Substance, then I
should be able to perceive it directly; even look-

ing at sense objects I should be able to perceive it.

Well, you know, in a way that was really very odd. How can you with the senses perceive the most refined being, the most subtle being, called God? Everybody, in all the books, has said that you cannot perceive the divine Reality by means of the senses or of the intellect; and as you learn more, you find that you are expected to undergo many different kinds of discipline in order to make your mind fit for such perception. But in those days ignorance helped. I didn't bother about those things. I said, if there *is* that Substance, instead of seeing only the sense forms, my eyes should be able to go beyond the sense forms and perceive that Substance directly. Well, it had a wonderful effect. I found myself continually trying to penetrate this barrier of forms.

You know there is a formula in Vedanta to the effect that the world of appearance is made up of name and form, while the reality is beyond name and form. Thus I am Reality plus name and form. 'Form' is what you see or perceive, that is, Reality as it is partially perceived through the senses. And 'name' is the idea that you have about It in your own mind. This formula makes Vedanta very simple if you are sufficiently intent upon it. The view that everything is Reality, divine Reality, plus name and form, is a wonderful way of speaking about the mystery of this world. Then, if you take the universe as a whole, you can say, "All these forms are nothing but mist floating over a luminous Being, hiding it, not allowing you to perceive it; nevertheless these forms are unconnected with the Reality. Form may hide Reality but cannot affect It."

Thinking these things helped me a great deal. I used to dwell on them for hours every day. I would analyze everybody. When I walked along the street, as soon as I looked at a person—and why only a person? Trees and cows, birds and beasts, whatever came before me—I would at once let my mind analyze and say, these are the form; beyond the form is the real Being. And my mind would try to penetrate the form in order to reach the real Being. I have found this practice very helpful. Therefore on many occasions I have said that you should try to look at things as they really are, even now, when you are functioning through the senses. After all, it is not only the senses that function in you; everything within you can function at the same time. As I just told you, they say you cannot perceive God with the eye of the body or with the eye of the mind; you have to have the eye of the Spirit in order to perceive Him. That is true. But who told you that you have to look only with the eye of the body or even with the eye of the mind? Why should you not also use the eye of the soul?

Combine all those things; then you will be surprised to find that which seems hidden in a person, the soul, is not *really* hidden. How can it be hidden? Its very nature is effulgent. What can hide it? If you say, "Well, it may be effulgent, but light can become hidden." No, not that kind of light; Spirit is all-powerful, nothing else has any power over it. So how can that light in any way be clouded by anything? By name or form or by whatever else—how can it be clouded? But you see, such is the way we function now: though the soul is there, we don't perceive it, and we take for granted that not perceiving it is the natural state of things, forgetting that in our state of ignorance everything we do is the opposite of what we should do. It is the soul, the effulgent Being, that should stand first before our eyes, but it is the last thing that comes to us.

Of course many would say, "No, we don't perceive any kind of spiritual substance anywhere. We see a person and we see his body; maybe we see also a little of his mind or we infer his mind, but beyond that we don't see anything. Who knows if there is a soul at all?" My feeling is that philosophy begins when you learn to look at things not as ordinary people look at them. I have often thought that it is really a false effort, anyhow one barren of results, to start with things as most people perceive them or even as science declares them to be. That is only one way of looking at the world. If you try to base a philosophy on it, such a philosophy will be still in the realm of ignorance. You see, when real knowledge comes, it is not that you get a new fact added to what you already know; it is that what you already know becomes revealed in an entirely different light. How do you know a person, a man? Various branches of knowledge study the subject of man; you learn things about human beings in various ways. True philosophy is not a summation of this knowledge, nor even something added to it out of your speculation upon it. No. It is an entirely different view of reality, which you discover through another kind of vision. But this vision cannot come to a person until he has subjected the mind to tremendous discipline.

Now, all of you have read some textbooks on Vedanta, and you know that they lay down certain conditions that must be met before anyone is accepted as a student of Vedanta. In India even now, if you were to go to an orthodox Vedantic teacher, he would not accept you as his pupil unless you had fulfilled all these conditions: first, perfect self-control, control over your senses and over your mind; second, you should not have any desire for enjoying pleasures either in this life or in lives to come or in heaven. Then, you must have a strong sense of the distinction between the real and the unreal; you should be able to put one thing against another, the real against what hasn't any substance, any reality. Your mind must have learned to look at everything in this way. Finally, there should be an intense desire to become liberated from the bondage of ignorance. These are the conditions you have to fulfill before you can be accepted by any orthodox teacher.

Of course, things have changed. You see, intellect has gone far ahead of life in almost every part of the world. We can think about most profound things, but we cannot live up to them at all. Our life has become undisciplined; our intellect is not satisfied with anything less than the highest philosophy. There has been this strange situation for quite some time. We know about many things, and we think things out because we want to be rational; then we also want to live a life in accord with our intellectual conviction. Yet the art of living so is a very strenuous art, and you cannot practice this art unless you have disciplined yourself severely, but that discipline we do not want to accept. I admit the old orthodox way is no longer possible; besides, books on Vedanta have been translated and published, and if you say, "Don't read them," no one will listen to you. Once I told a young man not to read certain books. So the first thing he did on going home was to gather those books and read them. You see, that is the attitude. You *will* read them, and there you have it. Yet if this gap between life and conviction can be filled, then we shall have an extraordinary generation of people, or generations of people, the like of which was never even dreamt of in the olden times. But this fact will always remain: if you study Vedanta and if its truth is to become a reality in your life, then you have to undertake spiritual discipline. And this, of course, is where religion comes in.

4

These, then, are the conclusions that I arrived at: that there is only one reality, the Spirit; that I am that Reality; and if I am that Reality, then I am not bound by this body or these senses or even by my mind—so I have to admit that I am infinite, I am limitless. How can there be anything outside me? If you say, "Now, Swami, that's no way to think: it sounds so awfully egotistical. How can you think that you are all there is and we are nothing? Are you really so majestic, so great, that you can say you are the whole of reality?" Yes, I can say that, but it is not egotism.

Egotism is itself a phase of the mind. You have read in Vedanta that the ego is one of the four aspects of the mind. You can realize a state when you actually see that the ego has nothing to do with you. In that state you can't be egotistic.

Egotism thrives on the recognition of other people with whom you can compare yourself and find yourself superior; without that, you cannot have any egotism. If you are the all, how can you make comparisons? In fact, you cannot even say 'I', because when there is only one reality, it becomes a silent entity. It cannot define itself, it cannot name itself, for all naming and defining belong to the mind. And if you are not the mind, if you are beyond it, if you are the ineffable Reality in which there is no definition and in which there are no terms, then what you are cannot be expressed in *any* way.

In Vedanta philosophy, as you well know, this Reality has been called the *Ātman*. *Ātman* is translated as the "Self"; It is conscious, in fact all-conscious. If you say, "We don't find ourselves to be all-conscious; our consciousness is limited, and even that limited consciousness fails sometimes, as when we have a fainting fit or when we fall deeply asleep," I admit that this may be so in your present state. You have not liberated your consciousness, and therefore you don't know what consciousness is in itself, what its true nature is. As our philosophers have pointed out, the very fact that you recognize that you fell asleep, or were unconscious, shows there was another consciousness remaining there and watching you become unconscious. After all, how do you know, when you wake up, that you fell asleep and didn't know anything? *How* would you know it if there were not also a witnessing consciousness within you? If you begin to think like this, a new world opens before you, and you do not find satisfaction in anything less. You continually try to break through the world of forms, to break through the world of ideas which you have inherited and which are rarely correct—certainly not correct in the highest sense.

I told you a little while ago that I used to say to myself, if the truth is there I should be able to see it, even with these eyes, and I made a continual effort to penetrate this barrier of forms. And I may say this, I was not unsuccessful. You can reach a state in which you look at things with these very eyes but you see something different from what you ordinarily see. The sense forms have stood aside and the true Reality—the spiritual Reality which everything is—becomes at once self-evident, directly perceived. You can do it, and that, really, is the only way to see.

Why do you think these senses, instead of seeing the Spirit, see Mr. David or Mrs. Smith? And then why do you add some long story— "Oh, she's a very quarrelsome woman, full of gossip," or "Oh, she's a wonderful lady." You look at a person and say, "He's a very egotistical man; look how ugly his nose is, look at his lips, look at his eyes." Why do you think you say all those things? It's because what you see is supported by ideas that you have in your mind, by what is called *name*. *Nāma-rūpa* they call it in Sanskrit. *Nāma* means name or, as I mentioned earlier, the words that indicate ideas, and *rūpa* means form—the outside objects we perceive. For every outside form you have a corresponding idea and word in your mind; and these two, name and form—or idea and thing—are tied together.

I am saying to you, following Vedanta, "Look upon everybody as an embodiment of God, or as God Himself." You may well say, "What a strange thing to ask us to do. Is everyone *really* God? How do I know that everything is God? What is the sense of following something which is so unrealistic?" Yes, in a way I agree with you there; one should not follow anything that is unrealistic. I have always been cautious about it. I have a profound suspicion of mere speculation. Western philosophers have indulged so much in speculation! They take whatever facts they can gather together and arrange them, and still they find many things missing. So through speculation they struggle to fill up the gaps, and presto! they have a system of philosophy. But no one can live by such a system of philosophy. It's a good exercise of the brain; but if you follow something that has no parallel in reality, you will find you are becoming more and more empty; you are living in a world of fantasy, and that is deadly. No one should live divorced from reality.

So you see, it is necessary that we actually *perceive* every person as God. And here is the clue to such perception: if you can change the idea that you have about a person, then your senses will see differently. You probably will not accept this. You will say, "You mean to say that if I change my ideas about a person, then instead of seeing that person I shall begin to see God?" That is *exactly* what I mean. It can be done, it has to be done, that is the only way we can go.

When you have associated certain ideas with a certain objective form, how are you sure that this association is correct? You look at a person and say, "Here is a thief." How do you know he is a thief? "Oh, I saw him entering a house and taking things away." All you saw was that the body of that person went there and the body functioned in this, that, and the other way, and then the body went surreptitiously out of the house. But is that the total man? You have only seen the function of the body. "Well, I saw in his eyes that furtive look; and he was full of greed. These things I saw in his mind." All right, so you have seen them. How much of the mind have you seen? And then beyond the mind what have you seen? Here is a total person to whom you have given the status of thief, or man, or whatever. But what about the other thing about which you do not know and about which you do not speak at all but which is most essential to this being whom you call man? If you could put all these three things together—body, mind, and Spirit—in one piece of knowledge without contradiction or conflict, I would say all right. But then you would not call that just man. The word *man* indicates a certain idea in your mind, and that idea does not include this immortal and infinite Spirit.

5

Here, then, is a profound question. What is the individual man—is there any such thing? If I am to speak about my philosophy in this connection, I must mention something—an idea that made a very deep impression on my mind; I still carry that impression, I still think it is true. You see, I feel even monistic Vedanta has fallen prey to a mistake. Even the great Shankara, who is recognized as the greatest monistic Vedantist, even he fell into that error. However, we think he spoke in this way not because he thought it final truth but just to help us. Every philosophy has to have a standpoint; philosophy certainly is not just transcendental; it tries to help people, to reach them where they are. Shankara took the standpoint of objective idealism—the standpoint of all men, all intelligent men. He started with what they think and perceive; and so he said that there are many beings, an infinite number of beings, and that these beings are really Spirit, but that they have, through ignorance, forgotten that fact. These beings have been endowed with a mind and a body, and they function through them. To this complex Shankara gave the name of *jīva*. *Jīva* is translated "individual self," that is to say, the Self individualized. It has become individualized by being encased in the mind and the body. And so it is this which is seeking knowledge, this individual; it is this which practices religion; it is this which tries to conquer ignorance; it is this which finds its identity with Brahman or God in the end. All of which seems awfully nice. It is so satisfying, all just right, true to our experience: "I am in that condition; I am a miserable individual; however, I want to conquer my misery." And Shankara goes on, "Now you do this and you do that, you discipline yourself through worship, meditation, and all. In course of time you will find that you are free from the bondage of the body and the senses and the mind. You will begin to realize that you are beyond these things and that you are pure Spirit; eventually you will find you are identical with God; all these things you will experience finally." All this time, if you think deeply, you will find you have no proof that there is any such strange animal as the *jīva*—no proof at all.

Oh, at one time I used to puzzle over this. I used to seek some justification in the world of experience for assuming there is such a thing as an individual. I came to the conclusion at that time, yes, there is at least one individual: that is myself. I still feel identified with the body and the mind; therefore I have to call myself an individual being. When I am called by a certain name, I respond to it; when a certain description is given of me, I recognize myself; if people say unpleasant things about me, I get annoyed. So I, at least, am an individual self. Then I came to the further conclusion that I am the only culprit. As regards you, how am I to know that there are individuals in you like that? All I find is that because I cannot perceive clearly, I see you all as having been endowed with bodies and minds, and I see these bodies and minds as different in quality and different in form. But that's *my* mistake; my senses and my mind are creating all this trouble. My senses perceive these appearances outside me—outside me because I have also endowed myself with one of these forms, and doing that has divided me, divided my real infinite being. So part of that real Self I see outside, part I see within myself. And I say to myself, "Well, it is my fault. If my senses were pure, if my mind were pure, if I were independent of the mind and senses, I would see only God everywhere; I would not find any trace of these so-called individuals or *jīvas.*"

I have always felt that this has been one of the stumbling blocks in our religious life or in our pursuit of Truth: we have assumed so many things without proof. I look at a person; what do I see? To begin with I see his appearance, his physical appearance; then through his eyes and his lips and his words and actions I begin to have an idea of the inner being, of the mental state; beyond that I don't see. How can I conclude that beyond that there is an ignorant person, a good or a bad man? What justifies me in thinking so? If you say that the inner person is the cause, that the mind and body are the effect, and that by seeing the effect we can determine the nature of the cause, then I ask, how do you know it is the cause? I say that the inner being does not produce the mind and does not produce the body. These things are not effects, they are just superimpositions made by my mind on what's before me. If a painter paints on the canvas all kinds of figures, do you mean to say that the canvas itself is the same color and the same form? It would be a great mistake to come to that conclusion. I say that beyond this body and beyond this mind there is an unlimited consciousness. If I cannot give any limit to this consciousness, then it becomes the infinite conscious Being, whether I am looking at a cow, or a cat, or a dog. These—cow, cat, dog—are all forms; form is made up of body and mind. But beyond this form is the real Being, and that real Being is the Divine Being. That is the conclusion I came to.

But you know, it is one thing to draw a conclusion from your reasoning and quite another thing to feel it instinctively as the truth. I may reason that a cow is not a cow, the cow is Brahman; a dog is not a dog, the dog is really Brahman; good man, bad man, young, old, all these are only on the surface; actually speaking, each is God Himself. It is one thing to read it, to speak in this way, to say, "I believe Brahman is the sole reality." It is quite a different thing to perceive it as such.

I used, therefore, to spend hours and hours correcting my thoughts. This thought—this way of looking at things, this erroneous way—has been in us for how many lives, who knows? And it is so deep-rooted that it is not easy to destroy. Yet it *must* be destroyed; it must be rooted out before we can see things correctly. I remember I had a very unusual experience at that time. My college life was over, and I had become a school-teacher for a short period. There was a cat and it had given birth to several kittens in our house. I remember one day I was alone and there was this mother cat and one of her kittens. I looked at the mother cat. I saw her face as luminous, lumi-

nous with divine light. I still remember that
experience. I did not have to reason it out. My
efforts had slowly succeeded in breaking the barrier. You see, what we have built up through our
error is so thick and so powerful that it takes a
long time and a very determined effort before we
can break through it. But slowly and slowly the
experience does come.

Let me give you an illustration. You can look
at a canvas and there find mountains, lakes, canyons, and the sky—everything painted in lifelike
manner. Looking at this picture you see profound depths and great heights, and yet it is
nothing but a thin piece of canvas, just a very
thin canvas. You can pick it up and take it away.
Then all the mountains, heights, and depths disappear. In the same way this world seems vast to
you, and it seems to arise from some profound
cause, or chain of causes. But that is just another
mistake, tracing everything to a cause.

To tell you the truth, when it comes to the
whole concept of cause, I am more in agreement
with the Buddhistic idea that things haven't any
real causal relation; they just succeed one
another. Of course, I am not a Buddhist. I don't
say that everything is momentary; momentari-
ness creates lots of trouble, philosophically. But
I do say that there is no intimate connection
between one event and another. One follows the
other, that's all. There is no real cause, there is

no real effect. Now, don't remind me that we have found that things are caused, that you can take a grain and put it in the ground and a little sprout comes out of it, that it then grows up and gives more grain. Yes, as long as you live on this level of thought, in this present order which seems so real to you, you will have 'causality'— although philosophers have cudgeled their brains without coming to any understanding of what is meant by 'causality.' However I am not speaking of this ordinary level, I am speaking of another order of perception. In that order of perception, body and mind do not come from the Spirit, though for their existence they are dependent upon it, just as the painted mountains and lakes and canyons depend upon the canvas. You could not paint all these things unless there was a canvas. Similarly, though these appearances are not *caused* by the pure Self, you could not see them unless the pure Self was there. I would not even use the word *support* for the Self—it is just that the forms cannot be perceived unless there is something on which the forms can be painted.

And so I persuaded myself that this is the only true way of thinking. I still think so. I still say that what order of reality I perceive is dependent on the condition of my own mind. If I am seeking the highest order of reality—and by highest I mean the transcendental order of reality, the

eternal order that is true for all times and not
dependent on a set of circumstances, where
knowledge is absolutely clear and not full of
confusions and darknesses and conflicts—then I
must deny all these things I have inherited from
my predecessors and learned from my contem-
poraries. I must repudiate the idea of the *jīva*, the
individual self. For, as long as I see that here is a
man and here is a bird and here is this and here is
that, as long as I govern myself with the popular
conventions, I shall condemn myself to ignorance. If I want to live up to truth, then not only
my perceptions, not only my behavior, not only
my expectations should be based on the fact that
everyone is that divine Reality, I must forever
live in the consciousness of It; I must not be
conscious of anything else.

6

From what I have told you, you no doubt have a
general idea of what my Vedantic outlook is.
Whether it will help the world in becoming
prosperous, whether it will tame the Russians is
not the concern of this philosophy. I can see
some of you becoming very pious: "What! You
haven't got any sympathy for the world? What
can be more important than to tame the Russians now? The whole world is going to be blown
to smithereens by their big bombs, and you in-

dulge in a philosophy that has nothing to do with all these urgent problems!" Philosophy and religion are not concerned with solving these economic or political or military problems. Religion has degraded itself by becoming interested in all these subjects. If you say, "Those are the problems of men. How can we ignore them?" I say, "Don't ignore them; but don't make the mistake of thinking that dwelling upon them is practicing religion." Religion has its function, and it is absolutely necessary for man. Man must become established in the consciousness of his own true Self. The more he does so, the more peace will come in the world, the more he will find he has solved the problems of his life and the problems of his fellowmen—if that is what he wants. But if you don't have that consciousness, you will make a mess of everything. The world will be like millions of madmen let loose from a lunatic asylum.

So religion has its own particular province and particular function. If we forget this function and let it take up other functions, we are thereby destroying religion, and that is what is happening in many places. Even in India the people have become so utilitarian in their outlook they sometimes say to you, "Now, what kind of religion is this? It does not take away poverty, it doesn't do this, it doesn't do the other thing." Well, religion never said it was going to give you money. That is not the function of religion. Here we are talking about philosophy and religion. Philosophy tries to determine what is the truth, what is the real, so that we can live up to that and forget all other nonsense. And religion requires that you make every effort to realize truth, to make truth actual in your experience—that is the function of religion. So this is my religious outlook: I say all this is Brahman, everything is God; and when you feel this—when you feel that your true nature is divine Reality—then you know how to live your life, you know how to treat others, you know what to strive for, you know what is the highest value.

One of our swamis once had a wonderful experience. One afternoon he went to meditate in the chapel of the monastery where he lived. Finished with his meditation, he saluted the Lord on the altar and was going out. As he came near the door he heard a voice, a silent voice from the altar, telling him, "I am the reality, I am the reason, I am the meaning, I am the value, I am the purpose, I am the fruition of everything." A most extraordinary experience! That is it. The world *appears* real because behind this fantasy of forms there is the existence of God. That gives the meaning to everything. If life seems to have a meaning, it is because behind life there is the presence of Divinity. That is the purpose of existence, too. If we don't go towards God, we defeat the purpose of existence. And that is the value: all the things that our heart seeks here—beauty, love, sweetness, joy, and peace—they are found in God, nowhere else. We think they are somewhere else, but they are not. Take God away, all of those things would disappear. Reality would become unreal, meaning would become meaningless, value—there would not be any. I thought that was a most wonderful experience. And the swami who had it, for a long, long time it remained in his mind, deeply impressed.

Yes, that's it. And when I say all this, I think I am on the sure ground of reason. That is to say, I am not ridden with contradictions. And I think thereby I come to a most satisfying religion as well. What can be more satisfying than to know that everything is transcendental Spirit, and to know that Spirit is the all? It is the reality; it is the truth; it is all the values. All the things that we seek exist in infinite measure in the Spirit. There is no other purpose to life. Know everything to be God, and everything will be fulfilled. For out of that knowledge come infinite love, infinite peace, infinite joy, infinite kindness and compassion, infinite service. And if you have all these, what more do you want?

WHEN THE MANY
BECOME ONE

The following lecture is of a somewhat different character from the two that precede it. In the earlier lectures, as the reader will have seen, Swami Ashokananda dwells on the philosophy and practice of Vedanta from a monistic standpoint. In this lecture he offers some of his own pertinent experiences. In some respects, "When the Many Become One" serves the preceding lectures as an illustration serves a book: it illumines the text, presenting, in at least some measure, the reality of what has been explained.

As the Swami remarks at the outset, the lecture was his first after a long illness; it was also, because of a subsequent long illness, the last public lecture he ever gave. It should be mentioned, however, that the small amount of editing the transcript has undergone was done under his supervision.

I DO NOT KNOW know how many of you are interested in a subject of this nature, but during the last several months I have thought about how the many become One a great deal. Probably most of you know that I was not well during this vacation time. In fact, I was desperately ill, and that is the reason I was not able to take up lectures, classes, and interviews after the vacation. During that period I dwelt often on experiences that I had had in days past, experiences in which I seemed to move from the manifold to the consciousness of the One and from which I derived a great deal of benefit and joy. As I looked back upon those days, and the days since in which that experience has from time to time repeated itself, I could not but think that these things were very important in my existence. Isn't it true, I thought, that everybody is seeking this One, although he may not say so in so many words? In his search, if he is succeeding he is happy. If he fails and then goes after other things which are only apparently the One but not really so, he will not be happy.

Yes, we are really seeking the One. Consciously or unconsciously, knowingly or unknowingly, we search for the One, oftentimes the false one, sometimes the real One. The real One, I have to confess, is difficult of access for most people. The One, as it were, has hidden Himself. There is a verse in the *Īśā Upaniṣad* that mentions this. The Upanishads, you know, are ancient books—some short and some long—in which the Indo-Aryans embodied their spiritual and philosophical findings. They were and still are regarded as exceedingly valuable. If the tradition is to be believed, those ancient people—boys and girls, young men, young women, even old men—all flocked to the forest retreats where these teachings were given by those who knew them. These truths were memorized, and they have come down to us in the original form. It can be truly said that they have not been adulterated but have been kept pure, and even today as you read these books you feel the ring and rhythm of those ancient people.

The *Īśā Upaniṣad* is one of the very ancient books, very short. Towards the end the teacher, says:

Hiraṇmayena pātreṇa satyasyāpihitaṁ mukham
Tat tvam pūṣann apāvṛṇu satyadharmāya dṛṣṭaye[1]

Hiraṇmayena pātreṇa satyasyāpihitaṁ mukham—"The face of Truth is covered by a golden disk." A golden disk has hidden the face of the Truth. Then he prays, *Tat tvam pūṣan apāvṛṇu*—"O Pushan, You who cherish and protect us, do remove this covering from Your face." Why? *"Satyadharmāya drṣṭaye"*—"So that I, whose religion is Truth, may see the Truth."

Isn't it true that this world is covered with a golden disk? Everybody wants the golden disk. Who doesn't want gold? It was only the other day that there was so much hurry and bustle about gold. All the idiots of this idiotic world have run after gold. But this wasn't the meaning really; the word golden wasn't meant here to symbolize wealth. Why, then, is the disk that hides the face of Truth called golden? I think you know the answer. If the moon were to see the earth, it would find it golden—certainly alluring—just as we find the moon golden and alluring when we look at it from our side. Everything looks golden and alluring from a distance. So this sage prayed, "Your face is covered with a golden disk. Do You remove it so that I may see the Truth." That is the fact: everything is alluring here; everybody is eager for the things of this world; but that is not seeing the Truth. You have to ask Him who is protecting you and the world to remove the golden disk which covers His face. And, you know, that is what we have been praying for; we may not recognize it, but that is always our prayer.

How is that disk to be removed? Of course, the common answer would be that we pray to God and He will remove the disk from His face. But that is not how it is done. You have to pray to God, but you have to make other efforts as well.

What do you have to do? You have to remove those things within you that make you see the golden disk over the face of everything. Why do we find this world so alluring and so charming? Because we are fools, and we want those things. The world looks so beautiful. As you outgrow childhood everything seems to tempt you, everything looks beautiful. That is what is called youth. Your body has matured, your senses have become stronger; the inner senses look upon everything through the outer senses, and everything looks tempting. So if you can remove this inner sense of glamour and do not pursue these temptations, the world will not look alluring. You might say, "Better to see something than not to see anything at all." Well, you will see something. You will catch a glimpse of the real golden color of the face of Truth.

I have told you on occasion that the time comes when your mind reaches a higher state. And the seat of that higher state, as I have often explained to you, is in the region of your heart. Most people live in the stomach level; then they don't see those higher things. But when you go beyond it and your mind reaches the level of the heart, you begin to have glimpses of light. Sri Ramakrishna said that when a person first has this vision of light, he is astonished and says,

"What is this! What is this!"—it is so unusual, so different from anything you see here. Neither the light of the sun nor of the moon nor of the lightning nor of fire nor of anything compares with the light that you see there. It is said that this is the first vision of the Light Divine. But that is not the end of it, that is just the beginning. You see more and yet more, until you recognize what this light is. You feel you have risen above the level of the body and of the senses; you feel you are not bound by them. You feel like a different person.

I told you that you do not reach that state until you have gone beyond your stomach. What a horrible thing to say! However, I think that is a simple way of saying that you are no longer borne down by the body, the body cannot conquer you any more; you are free of it. And it is in that state that you begin to see the face of Truth, or, to put it another way, you begin to have the sense of the One; you begin to think you are no longer bound by the many. I have told you that you perceive the many and are bound by it because you are in this lower plane—they call it the plane of the navel, *nābhi*. (The navel, they say, is the center of that plane; so an area above it also belongs to it.) When you are in that level, you perceive the manifold world and feel its attraction.

You have noticed what people do: they invite

somebody to dinner. They eat, they drink, they talk, they dance, they sing. It is not just a matter of eating a luscious dinner. All these activities are bound up together, and people think they are most wonderful things to do. They don't know that if they continue in this, very soon they go down and down, further and further. They go out to dinner; they invite others to dinner, round and round; and if they cannot please, they feel very unhappy about it. Well, I needn't say more. The whole world is doing these things.

But when you progress from the navel area towards the heart area, you feel that your world is changing, and you begin to feel the One. How do you feel the One? The One is felt like a thread in a necklace of pearls. Just as a thread holds all the pearls together, similarly the sense of oneness holds the whole world together. This sense grows; you begin to be conscious of the One more and more.

Suppose you meditate. You have gone into that state where you like to meditate on the One. When you finish your meditation, you find a sense of oneness pervading everything. You feel it in your heart, and your heart feels in union with the unity that you feel within the world.

I remember a time at Belur Math when there had been the worship of the Lord Shiva. Monks particularly worship Lord Shiva. They hold four worships, in four periods of the night. After they have finished the last worship, meditated, and so on, the night has come to an end, and they go to the Ganges to bathe. You feel wonderful in the morning. All day long you have prepared for that night of worship and meditation. You don't eat anything, don't sleep, don't drink, don't do any of your ordinary work. And when night comes you start your first worship, then the second and third and fourth worships. At dawn, after you bathe, you are allowed to eat something. Swami Shivananda was the head of the Order at that time. He had become pretty old and rarely could come down the stairs, but on this occasion he was brought down in a chair. He looked around and said, "What a wonderful time! The whole world has become steeped in the being of Shiva. Everywhere the world has become filled with the presence of Shiva." Of course, he could say that: he was a very great saint; very unusual he was. He felt that, and he mentioned it. And we wondered, "What must have been the experience of one who could speak so feelingly about the presence of Shiva everywhere!" Yes, that is it. You reach a state where you feel the One everywhere.

You see, this is our whole philosophy—to perceive the One in the many, not to perceive the many alone. Poets may sense it and write beautiful poems about it. There was a great poet in Bengal, Rabindranath Tagore. I have read his books from time to time all my life. He was probably one of the greatest poets the world has produced. You may not know that, because you have read only some of his poems in translation. But he wrote volumes and volumes of poetry. He himself said, "I never fake any feeling. I write as I feel." He also speaks of this unity a great deal. You may interpret it according to your own feeling. You may take it as something he has not been able to perceive to the same extent as saints and sages—though in his later life he became very saintly. But just the same you can read and very much enjoy his poems. I became acquainted with his works when I was in high school, and a friend of mine and I used to read them. I must confess I did not feel them as intensely in those days as I came to feel them in later years, but we enjoyed them very much. Then as time went on, we began to appreciate in his poetry this sense of the One. There is a long poem I was reading only the other day, in which he prays, "Mother Earth, take me back to thyself. I have to become mingled with your being, not separated in the slightest." That is the sum and substance of the poem, but of course he expressed it in beautiful language.

Well, you come to feel like that. You feel like becoming one with the whole universe. You do not want to be separate from anything but to become one with everything. Then, in being one with everything—in that very experience—everything changes for you and you change for everything.

There was a time when I liked that idea very much. I had finished my education in the university and was living in a small town. It was a very unusual kind of place, with the habit of becoming inundated with floods. Every year a good part of the town would be under water, as was the neighboring land for miles and miles all around, and sometimes the water would be ten, twelve, or twenty feet deep. For several months the water remained there, until the autumn came; then it would disappear. Slowly it would disappear. Well, it was a beautiful thing to see. Here and there you would see trees standing in the water. Maybe you could see small villages floating in water. You wouldn't see anything else. I made a habit in those days of going into the back yard of the house where I lived. From there I could see miles and miles of this water, and there I would sit. There was no rain at that time. I would sit there and lose myself in the utter oneness of these undivided waters. No waves there; the water not moving. And there was the sun. I looked towards the east, and for miles and miles I would see only water in which the blue sky and the sun were reflected. And then I would lose the sense of outerness; that sense of an outer world at which I was looking would go away, and the sense of oneness that this vast water created would pervade the mind, saturate the mind, and somehow overwhelm the mind. For two hours, three hours I would sit like that, and I would be in what you may call a sort of meditation. I would lose myself in this sense of oneness pervading everywhere; I would not remember even my own physical existence.

Then it would be time to bathe. There was no lack of water there! After I had bathed, I would meditate on the sun, and that meditation was also of a peculiar character. I wore eyeglasses even in those days, and I would take them off and hold them so that the sun would shine on the glass. The sun would appear small in the lens, but it was a very convenient symbol for meditation, and I would lose myself in that meditation for a long time.

That also was good, and those months when I lived there were very profitable. My mind used to go deep, as day after day, day after day I would sit in the open seeing these vast waters—endless, calm, quiet. That was certainly something to meditate on, and that meditation did not leave me. Afterwards on many occasions I lost myself in that kind of meditation under different circumstances.

You see, at first you take something outside on which you meditate. Then a time comes when you do not have to take anything outside;

an inner feeling comes, and you lose yourself in that. But let me tell you again: the essence of the whole thing is to lose the consciousness of the outer world, of sense things. If you don't do this, you cannot go deep within.

Now, you have heard about other kinds of meditation or read about them and thought about them. One of the very common ways—and I do not mean common in the sense that it is of no use—is meditation on one of the forms of God. There are devout Christians who like to meditate on Christ, and Buddhists who meditate on Buddha. Among the Hindus there are many who meditate on other forms of the Deity. Hindus delight in having discovered many divine forms for the purpose of meditation. You may say, "Oh, all these gods! We don't like that." But whether you like it or not, you must admit that since men are so various, it will be a delight to them to have a choice of various ways of meditation. If you don't like one form of God, you can take another and meditate on that. Some of these forms may express to you great states of being. Christ is a state of being; Buddha is a state of being; many Hindu deities also are states of being. You pick one. The teacher will describe that form and the way you should think of that deity. Then as you dwell on that form, your mind gradually becomes immersed in it.

Long ago I read the *Vishnu Purana*, one of our

old Sanskrit books. In it there is a description of a meditation, a long description. I won't go into the details, but it is one of the ways of meditation which are mixed with devotion or love: you meditate on Krishna, because he is the embodiment of love. You meditate on him, and his form becomes real and brings to you not only the consciousness of the One Being, of which the whole world is an expression, but also a sense of beauty, a sense of love, and you feel the whole universe is really an expression of this Love, this Inner Being. That is a wonderful meditation. If you practice it, you will derive a great deal of spiritual benefit from it. That is the path of devotion in which most people of the world are interested and which most people want to follow.

Various other ways of meditation are taught and practiced. Of all these, some say the supreme path is the path of knowledge, in which you do not think of any object but dwell on your own Self or Brahman as the all, and thereby you attain to a very high state.

I think the kind of meditation I spoke of having was meditation on Brahman; that is to say, on God without form, the Formless. I did not try to see any form. I tried to feel the presence of this One Being in myself and in all the things around me. I liked doing that, and I think I succeeded to a little extent. So that is one way you can meditate, and after a time you will find that you have become separated somewhat from the body; you no longer feel that you are physical; you feel that the real Being is within you, and not only within *you* but in others as well. You will perceive the same Being in everyone—in you, in me, in everything: human beings, subhuman creatures, living and even nonliving. You can perceive that He permeates everything.

If you don't attain to that state, how can you find any peace? Can you find peace if you are separate from everything? There is a beautiful passage in one of the old Upanishads—the *Bṛhadāraṇyaka Upaniṣad.*[2] Swami Madhavananda has given this translation: "The brāhmin ousts one who knows him as different from the Self. The *kṣatriya* [the warrior] ousts one who knows him as different from the Self. The worlds oust one who knows them as different from the Self." It goes through a whole list: "The gods oust one who knows them as different from the Self. The beings oust one . . ." and so on. That is a tremendous statement. What is the meaning—if you think the brāhmin is different from the Self, that brāhmin will oust you? It is a fact that if you think yourself separate from any person, that person will make you small. Whatever you think is outside of you has the effect of making you small and limited. Isn't it true? If I meet some people and I fear them and I think that they are outside me and so on, what will be the effect of that thought on me? I certainly would be affected by this limitation that I impose upon myself.

There is a wonderful story in connection with this. Shortly after Swami Vivekananda had returned from the West in 1897 and had gone to Calcutta, he received a message from a friend of his, saying, "I have a peculiar disease. I am just wearing out. I am all the time in bed and cannot get up. Would you kindly come and see me? Not because I want any cure, but because I have known you, and I have heard you have returned from the West and I should be very glad to see you." So Swami Vivekananda at once sent a message, yes, he would go. The moment he entered the man's room he began to recite that passage from the Upanishad. He did not explain it, but such was the effect of this recitation that the man began to feel a new energy coming into his body and his mind, and he sat up and said, "Swamiji, I feel stronger than ever." And, as it happened, he was cured. He became like a new person.

Of course, Swami Vivekananda had great power; the real meaning of the verse went into the heart of the man, and he lost the idea that he was separate from this one and from that one; he became all alive. That is what happened to him.

Sometimes similar things happen to people. If

you are afraid of the world, if the world has limited you, circumscribed you, if you feel bound by the world or anything in this world, then consciously try to think that everything is Brahman, everything is divine, that nothing is outside you and nothing can affect you; you also are Brahman, you also are divine. Keep that consciousness, and you will find you have become a changed person. That is what you have to practice.

In one of the books of our philosophy, it is said, "Do not think that you are separate from anything. Whatever you think you are separate from will circumscribe you and bind you. Think that you are one with all, and you will feel free."[3] That is the true sense of oneness, but do not for a moment think that it can be derived by any superficial practice. Real things are not on the surface. That is the horrible mistake you people make in this country. You talk of great things, good things, but you think all these things are floating on the surface and all you have to do to attain them is to be superficial. No. That is a great mistake. Only the great can achieve the great. Only the deep can achieve the deep. If you say, "It seems to me the cure is more difficult than the illness," I shall ask why you think you have not deep power within you. Why should you have that idea? Why should you be superficial and think that that is your nature? That is where you are committing suicide. You are deep, profound. Try to be deep and profound and see if you cannot find deep and profound truth within yourself. You have to practice those things. If you become superficial, you will become like dust that is being scattered by the wind. You won't be anything better than that.

So I say if you want great things you should be very thoughtful about those things and should go deep where they are. The fact is that when you go deeper and deeper you are not far off from the Oneness of which I have spoken. The many disappears and becomes the One. Do you know what word we use for the perception of the One? We call it a state of *samādhi. Samādhi* means a state of profound meditation. You talk a lot about meditation nowadays, but do you know what meditation is? Meditation is very profound in its true nature. When you reach that state, there comes a deep sense of oneness within you. You feel one with everybody.

There is the story about Sri Ramakrishna. He was seated in his room, and outside his room a man was walking on the lawn, and he felt that the man was actually walking on his heart. He began to cry in agony, and a nephew who attended upon him came and asked, "Uncle, what is the matter?" He said, "Somebody has been walking on my chest." Of course the nephew didn't believe it. He did not see any man walking on his chest. Then Sri Ramakrishna explained how it was.

As you know, he lived in a temple on the bank of the River Ganga. Another day he set up a great cry; so the nephew came to see what was the matter, and he said, "Oh, somebody is beating me." The nephew ran to the river and found a boatman beating another boatman. The effects from this beating had appeared in Sri Ramakrishna—there were welts on his back. He had attained to that state of oneness in which he felt these things physically—not always, of course, but on many occasions. That is a fact of oneness; you feel that oneness. Even if you don't feel it in this physical way, you feel it in other ways. You feel oneness with somebody, and if he is suffering, you feel it.

This is not just talk. Long ago there was a discussion amongst some scholars in England. The question was, can anybody take the suffering of another? There were many arguments to prove that one cannot; you may say it, but you cannot actually do it. But there were also arguments that a few can really feel the sufferings of others, and take them upon themselves. Yes, that is the fact. When you lose your bondage to your own body and little self and become free of them, then you can indeed take somebody else's suffering on yourself. There have been such cases. Great saints and sages have realized that state, and people have spoken of those things. You, also, can realize that sense of oneness, but you are not really looking for that kind of oneness. What you really want is to have the experience of Oneness where you are no longer bound to the world of the many. The world of the many in itself is nothing; you want to go beyond it and make yourself one with the One which is at the heart of everything and is the root of everything. The world is based on this One. The manifold world exists on the foundation of this profound Unity. When you have made yourself one with that Unity, you have reached the very heart of the universe. That is what you want, and that is what you can do. I have no doubt that if you try you will surely realize that Unity.

1. *Īśā Upaniṣad*, 15.
2. *Bṛhadāraṇyaka Upaniṣad*, 2.4.6.
3. E.g., *Vivekacūḍāmaṇi*, 339.